A

Meditation

PRIMER

by Sokuzan

SokukoJi Buddhist Community Publications
33 Anderson Ct.
Battle Creek, MI 49017
www.sokukoji.org

KDP edition

ISBN: 9798673904022

Front cover design: excerpt of watercolor *The Six Realms* by Sokuzan

Back cover design: ink *Untitled Line Drawing* by Sokuzan

Dedicated to My Root Teacher
The Vidyadhara
Chögyam Trungpa Rinpoche,
Dorje Dradul of Mukpo

and

My Zen Master
Kobun Chino Roshi

CONTENTS

Introduction

This small book of talks arose because there seemed to be a need to express and repeat what shikantaza, or *just basically sitting*, is all about. Sometimes this *just basically holding still and looking* is preceded by creation or formation practices as in the Vajrayana Tibetan Buddhist traditions—creation/completion or forming complicated mandalas, images, deities, seed syllables, and doing mantras before one eventually dissolves those images back into oneself and rests in the completion stage called mahamudra or dzogchen.

In shikantaza, the creation part is your life—stories, images, and forms that you have been creating all day long. The completion stage is just observing, resting in space. You might need a lot more of this—just holding very still and seeing what arises without adding to it— very difficult to do because when we sit down and hold still, we see just how much we add. Rather than realize this as a necessary stage, we start to doubt ourselves thinking, "There's something wrong. I need to do something differently. I need to do this. I need to do that."

From my point of view, having done both creation/completion stages in the Kagyu and Shambhala Tibetan traditions and shikantaza or zazen in the Soto Zen tradition, I feel that, though one may need to go to the creation/completion stages of the Vajrayana traditions, it may not always be necessary to do that. And only *you* will really know.

So this little book is meant to reinforce, repeat, and help you dig a nice, deep groove—in the awareness of how to do this, in the recipe of how to do this, in the protocol of how to do this. *Just simply sit and observe.*

Please enjoy these talks, and stay in touch.

~Sokuzan

March, 2014

Meditation Instruction

"Poem"

Sit down
or stand up.
Walk around.
Hate yourself.
Love yourself.
Ignore yourself.
Eat candy.
Judge your neighbor.
Take off your clothes.
Sing something.
Eat something.
Wring out your washcloth.
Cancel your trip.
Plan a meal.
Plan to plan.
Wreck your car.
Lymph your node.
Eat five radishes.
Play the lottery.
Like something.
Hate something.
Realize something.
Jump right.
Jump left.
Stop jumping.
Live normally.
Live outrageously.
Leave the room.
Arm yourself.

Disarm yourself.
Come to no conclusion.

Forget everything I said.

Just Observe. . .

Meditation Instruction #1

"The Train of Thought."

Please face the wall.

Place your hands either on your knees or with the left hand on top of the right, thumbs just barely touching, forming an oval between your thumbs and first fingers. Either way is fine. Hold the back very, very straight without being rigid as if a string were pulling you upward by the top of your head—a very imaginative pull from the top of your head to straighten out your spine. Here again, not to be rigid but just to be very straight and very attentive to whatever is occurring in the body and the mind. Just observing.

Like sitting in a train station, you are watching the trains come and go—you could say, the "train of thought" coming and going. Don't board the train. And if you find yourself spontaneously getting on the train of thought and going into a memory of the past, daydream of the future, judgments, evaluations, hope and fear, little stories about yourself and your life, about what you are doing, about what you should do, about what you should have done, what you shouldn't have done. *Please*, do not meddle with those stories. Don't stop them. Do not fuel them. And do not look away from them. Just observe. You are glued to that bench in the train station for a few moments. Just observe.

If you are holding extremely still, very still without being rigid, with all of your senses open, then for you personally, *you personally*—not the person next to you—whatever arises in your mind is exactly what you need to see *at this particular place* in your lifetime, this very moment in the whole process of birth, aging, sickness, and death. Just observe.

If you really see fundamentally not only on the cushion but in your everyday life, if you really see fundamentally what this is, you will never make another decision again. You will never have a fork in the road. You will see completely and totally what it is you need to do at each moment. Without hope and fear. Completely. Thoroughly. You will be genuine. You will be yourself. Just observe. Do this for a few years. You can't change the course of a comet by blowing on it. You have to *be* the comet. You have to fully embody who you are—all of your negativity and all of your positivity, all of your thoughts, emotions, dreams, nightmares. Fundamentally and totally, *be genuine!* Don't deceive yourself. And when you deceive yourself, be aware that you are deceiving yourself.

Just observe. (Bell)

Meditation Instruction #2

*"Thank You Very Much. I Have No Complaint
About Anything Whatsoever."*

Please face the wall.

What we are doing here is controlling something that we
seem to have control over: the body. We are doing
something that people in general do not ever do other
than perhaps when they're sleeping. This is called
shikantaza in the Zen tradition, and it means "just
sitting." Just completely being here, simply, with
nothing extra.

So hold the body very, very still and endeavor to observe
what arises in the six sense fields. Sense of touch: how
this feels. Sense of taste: how this tastes. Sense of smell:
how this smells. Sense of sound. Anything that comes is
welcome. Sense of seeing. Just this simple space in

front of you is completely generous by being there, completely giving you everything. Just observe. Look at this wall or out this window, depending on where you are, or across the room, and just observe. Please—just observe.

Whatever comes, no matter how ragged, ragtag, or crippled the thoughts are that come and go—please, just observe. If you get really upset, just observe. Do not try to be peaceful. If you get really excited or happy, just observe. Do not add your stamp of approval. Please—it is not about getting over your emotions, your thoughts, your memories. It is not about getting rid of anything at all. This may surprise you. I'm afraid that the ears, nose, tongue, body, mind that you entered this particular existence with are yours.

So what's being said here is just be genuine. Be completely, thoroughly, and totally in your seat, and observe whatever arises. And with the attitude, with the complete understanding that may be put in this way:

"Thank you very much. I have no complaint about anything whatsoever. Thank you very much. I have no complaint about anything whatsoever." Even your rising complaints have no complaint about. Whatever arises out of this space we call the mind is completely and totally perfect as it is *regardless* of how heart wrenching it can be.

Please, just observe. Be genuine. In this way, sitting on this cushion, if only for a few moments or for several days, we have the opportunity to return to our original nature, our true nature—who we actually are. Holding the body very still without being rigid, all the senses are open. Whatever is arising at this very moment is exactly what you need to see. Don't accept it. Don't reject it. Don't look away. Just observe. Don't pull it into your lap. Don't throw it out the window. Don't change the subject. Whatever comes toward you, receive it. Whatever leaves you, say goodbye.

As it is. (Bell)

Meditation Instruction #3

"Don't Refuse Your Life."

Please face the wall.

The instruction goes like this: Hold the body very, very still without being rigid. Hands can be either on your knees in resting-the-mind mudra or in your lap with left hand placed over the right, thumbs slightly touching forming an oval in cosmic mudra. There's really no correct way to do it, but whichever way you decide to use, use it for awhile rather than go back and forth.

Holding the body very, very still—it's like a string pulling you up by your head towards the ceiling then relaxing into it slightly. It's about being relaxed but not too relaxed. The emphasis here is on just observing. In fact, this practice could be called "observing" rather than meditation because it is fundamentally just that.

Conventionally, we do not really observe—we observe for just a second, and then we jump to conclusions. We jump to evaluations. We name. We select. We decide. We evaluate. We choose. Picking and choosing, picking and choosing. Our lives get so uncomfortable because we refuse our life. We actually refuse the life that is presented to us.

When you sit down and begin to observe who this is, what the situation is *fundamentally*, then slowly, over time, we begin to return to our original nature which is complete sanity. Complete Buddhanature. Complete perfection without a second opinion. If you understand this, if you see what is true for yourself, you'll no longer have any questions about anything other than "What's for supper?"

So shikantaza is just sitting, holding very, very still. If you're facing the wall, your gaze is straight ahead. If you're facing the center of the room, which we often do —in fact, as we always do before we begin the morning service or sutra chanting—then your gaze would be down towards the floor. Your head is still erect, but your gaze is down towards the floor rather than out in space in front of you.

Holding the body very still, just observe. Whatever arises in the six sense fields—sense of taste, sense of touch, sound, sight, smell, thinking—all of that, just observe. No little comments, no post-it notes on anything that arises. Just observe. Like watching clouds in the sky. Fundamentally interesting—some are large, some are small, some are dark, some are light, some are stretched out, some are fluffy and puffy like your thought patterns. But you should take the attitude in this practice that, just like clouds, thoughts are *none of your business*.

"If you do nothing to thoughts, they will do nothing to you."*

So just sit here. As it is. (Bell)

*Quote from Bardor Tulku

Meditation Instruction #4

"Like Fish In A Pond, You Can't Control Thoughts."

Please face the wall.

Once again, hold the body very, very still without being rigid. All the senses are open, in particular the eyes. Look directly ahead at the wall that is in front of you. The basic thing to remember as we sit holding very still is to just observe. You're just observing. Just observing. Rather like watching clouds in the sky. Thoughts just come and go. Emotions. Feelings. Memories. Daydreams about the future. Recollections about the past. Judgments. Evaluations. Whatever. Just like clouds going by—rather none of our business, really. Take that attitude towards thought patterns and slowly, over time, begin to see thoughts as they actually are. Formations coming and going, neither good nor bad nor neutral. Just observe.

Sometimes we use the image of fish in a pond. They swim this way. They swim up. They swim down. They may be orange. They may be black. They may be white. They may be any combination of colors or patterns. They may be going in any direction quickly, slowly. Very much like thought patterns. You really can't control fish. You really cannot control thoughts.

But what we *can* do is just observe thought patterns as they come and go. We see the contrast between them. Some are rough and rugged and have ragged edges. Some are smooth and flowing, and there is not a sharp edge anywhere. They're very soft. Just observe. See the texture of your six sense fields including the mind. There is texture everywhere. Texture in how the body feels. Texture in what is in front of you. The wall. Texture. There is texture in the sound of the voice you are listening to. The voice that goes up or goes down and the spaces between the words, the syllables, and also the sound of the air conditioner running. Texture. Texture in the breath as it comes and goes. Just observe.

If you are holding very still and endeavoring to just observe, almost in a scientific way—very similar to a forensic approach, just looking at what is there, just looking at that, just observing—in this way we strengthen the awareness. We are able to see more and more clearly what is actually occurring not only on the cushion but in post meditation in our everyday life. We are able to see very clearly what this is fundamentally. This is the sitting practice of meditation. Shikantaza as it is called in Japanese. Or "just precisely this."

As it is. (Bell)

Meditation Instruction #5

"Don't Adjust."

Please face the wall.

After a full day of moving around, thinking this, thinking that, feeling this, feeling that, having lots of emotions, thoughts, memories, plans for the future, regrets about the past. Whatever may be arising moment by moment. In our daily life, we generally make adjustments, refuse some things that come up, push some things away, add onto things our opinions, ideas, judgments, evaluations. We do this spontaneously without even reflecting so much as a little bit. We just keep adding on, adding on, subtracting, dividing, doing all kinds of meddling with our mind.

But here in the last hours of the day we sit down, hold still. Just let everything settle. We don't try to make it settle. We don't have a discussion about how fast it's settling. We don't evaluate. We don't do anything at all in particular other than observe what is occurring. Moment by moment by moment. If you have intense negative feelings, emotions, just observe. If you have positive feelings, emotions, ideas, evaluations, just observe. Don't agree with anything that arises. At the same time, don't disagree. Just like looking at clouds, we don't really agree with them or disagree. We just observe. We don't look away. In this way, we train our mind to slow down and see the truth for ourselves.

So whatever is arising for you at this very moment, if you are holding still with all of your senses open, and your attitude is one of observing—in other words, *what* is this? *What is this? S*ee what this is moment by moment in any of the sense fields including the mind. Just observe.

See what it is as it is. (Bell)

Meditation Instruction #6

"Shikantaza."

Please face the wall.

Once again, simply put, hold the body very, very still without being rigid. Hands can either be in your lap left over right with thumbs slightly touching or they can be on your knees. Look directly ahead at the wall, the texture of whatever is in front of you. Look right directly at that. Listen for any sounds. Listen to the sound of the air conditioner. The birds. At the present moment—my voice. Listen to the texture of everything. Feel gravity pulling you down towards your cushion. Feel your clothes covering your body. The uncovered areas are slightly cooler than the areas that are covered. Notice that contrast. How things look. How this feels, and how this sounds. Very, very simply. No additions. No post-it notes on your thoughts. No commentary on anything that arises. Whatever arises is just precisely this. As it is with nothing added. Your acceptance, your rejection, your ignorance is beside the point. Just observe.

Shikantaza, or *just precisely this*. Just precisely this, precisely. Do not deviate one way or the other. And if you spontaneously find yourself wandering, stepping off, stepping up, stepping down, stepping sideways, moving this way or that, just observe. Only observe. Holding the body very still without being controlling or rigid, just observe. Like sitting on the banks of a stream. Leaves have fallen into the water. They are floating by—just like your thoughts. They come in front of your awareness, float through your awareness, and they float out leaving not a trace. Curled up leaves. Flat leaves. Green leaves. Brown leaves. Sometimes we'll even see fish if we look deeply into the water. Just observe. We may see contrast, but it does not point to something else. It is just that. Just dark. Just light. Thoughts are like that. They are just heavy, strong,

If you are here and endeavoring to hold very, very still with all the senses open, whatever arises in the six sense fields—including the mind—is exactly, precisely what you need to see at this very moment. There is nothing to correct. There is nothing to adjust. There is just this.

As it is. (Bell)

Meditation Instruction #7

"Completely Starting Over."

Please face the wall.

Each time we walk up to our cushion or chair and bow, then turn outward towards the Sangha and bow, take our seat, turn and face the wall. Each time we do this, *every* time we do this, we are completely starting over. This is quite a bit different from other skills, practices or information we learn: acquiring, acquiring, acquiring. This practice is a little different—in fact, it is quite a bit different.

Each time we sit down, we lose. Each time, we lose our temporary face, our temporary clothing, temporary skin and body. Our mirror image—we lose that. It just goes away. Unless, of course, we hang onto it. If we are trying to control, keep something back, hold onto something, get somewhere, build something up. If we are doing that, then we may not be just here, just present, just at a loss.

So what's being recommended here is shikantaza, a Japanese word that means *just precisely this.* Just precisely this. Exactly this, just sitting. Something we rarely do unless we're asleep: hold completely still. In fact, when we're asleep, we're not holding totally still. We just don't have much of a physical agenda. But here, if we do have an agenda, we sit down and observe how we don't particularly want to be here. Now, you might say, "But I do want to be here. I came here to meditate."

But fundamentally look. Use the awareness. Let whatever occurs when you hold completely still, let whatever occurs *occur.* Let it happen. Don't object. And if you object, don't object to the objection. In other words, don't double up on your negativity. One negativity is clean enough. If you have two, which means second thoughts, don't do it. But if you do it, don't have third thoughts. And if you have those, don't have fourth thoughts. Do you follow me?

What I'm saying is *just this*. Always return to square one. Ctrl/Alt/Del. Right here. Right now with nothing happening. A blank screen—or not. Maybe the screen is filled with zombies. Maybe the screen is filled with schmooze. Maybe the screen is filled with acolytes. Maybe the screen is filled with your last meal. Maybe there's nothing there. Just observe. This is the key word here. Just completely, totally give yourself over to this wall. What is in front of you—just observe.

Observe the texture of the wall. Observe the space intervening between your eye organs and the wall itself. Don't ignore anything. Include, include, include. Just observe. If you see you're excluding, observe that. That is actually including. You're including the excluding. We have to be very, very generous here. We have to be the giver, the receiver, and the gift all at once. If you see that, everything vanishes. But you won't know it. If you know it, then it hasn't vanished. Just observe. Holding the body very still, hands either on your knees or in your lap, left over right with your thumbs barely touching, in cosmic mudra, just observe.

Just observe. (Bell)

Meditation Instruction #8

"Whatever Arises Is Just What You Need To See."

Please face the wall.

If you're holding the body still without being rigid with all of your senses open and you are endeavoring to just observe, then whatever arises in the six sense fields, including the mind, *whatever* arises, *whatever* arises is exactly what you need to see at this very moment. There is nothing to correct. If you think there is, you're wrong.

And no, I'm not correcting you! (Bell)

Meditation Instruction #9

"Hold Very Still And See What Continues To Move."

Please face the wall.

Being busy all day long there are thoughts coming and going, activities, trying to start this, trying to stop that, endeavoring to understand more clearly what is occurring to us, what is occurring outside in relationships, and what is occurring inside in the ruminations that we make all day long—constant little comments on everything that occurs. When we come in and sit down in front of this wall, sit on this cushion, hold this posture very, very still and very precisely, in this way, *in this way*, we let everything slow down. Everything just slowly comes to a stop. This is shikantaza—*just precisely this*.

When you endeavor to do this, you are able to hold very still. You are able to hear quite well, see quite well, feel, taste, smell, and even think quite clearly, quite well. And what we notice when we hold very, very still is some things keep moving. Even the body held very still will continue to move, continue to breathe. Heart continues to beat. Blood flows. Slight movements happening all the time. Very, very slight—we notice them through contrast. We also notice that which continues to move and whose very nature is movement is the mind itself. Completely moving this way and that, up and down, back and forth, tracking this, searching out that, analyzing this, removing, replacing, adjusting, correcting, crediting—on and on.

And what is being said here is hold very, very still. Hold everything still you can in a gentle way. But if it can't be held in that way, then just observe. The mind will continue to rise up and fall away. Thoughts will appear and vanish. So just observe. Keep it very, very simple.

As it is. (Bell)

Meditation Instruction #10

"Thoughts Like Birds In The Blue Sky Of Your Mind.."

Please face the wall.

As we're sitting here doing nothing in particular except holding the body very still without being rigid or controlling—just very gently holding ourselves in a static position—as we do this, we will notice through contrast what continues to move. The diaphragm continues to move. Some muscles begin to move slightly. Eye blinks. Movement of the tongue inside the mouth slightly. If you need the instruction, the tongue should be on the roof of the mouth. This will handle any excess saliva.

Holding the body very, very still without being rigid or controlling, we just observe that which holds still—the body—and that which continues to fluctuate, vacillate, or search. Just observe this. Don't try to adjust, modify, or stop control of anything that is in motion. Anything that is in motion should be just observed like a bird flying through the sky. A bird is basically completely visible, completely stands out against the blue sky, the clouds. But it is none of your business. You have nothing to do with it. You have no sayso about it whatsoever. The bird may land. It may fly higher. It may fly lower. It may disappear. The only thing you are doing here is just observing.

So as thoughts fly through your mind, through the blue sky of your mind like birds, just observe. They may fly quickly or slowly. They may waver this way or that. They may glide. They may pump their wings. Just let the thoughts do whatever they want to do. Don't resist them. Don't accept them. And don't look away from them or ignore what is moving. Just observe.

In this way, the sitting practice of meditation called shikantaza, or *just precisely this*, as it is—in this way, we strengthen that which sees. We strengthen the awareness. Just being aware, we are not necessarily taking away from the thinking process, we are just not fueling it with more comments, criticism, judgments, appreciations. We're not feeding or fueling that process by adding anything to it. Later on in your post meditation, your everyday life when you are not meditating, this kind of process happens all the time. Cranking things up, slowing them down. Evaluating. Judging. Condemning. Accepting. Appreciating. Depreciating. We constantly meddle and try to manipulate our minds.

As meditators, we are doing none of that. And If we are doing that, what do we do? We just observe that. Don't meddle with the meddler. Just observe. Simplify. Completely and totally be as present as you can without an agenda other than hold the body very still and observe that which continues to move. In this way we begin to see the truth for ourselves.

As it is. (Bell)

Meditation Instruction #11

"Always About Awareness, Always About Contrast."

Please face the wall.

Here we are again, sitting down, slowing everything down. Observing our mind, slowly winding down, and coming to a rest. Body and mind are separated but fundamentally not separate. As the body is held still, without being rigid, the mind and thought processes slowly settle down.

If they do not, don't add anything to that other than the contrast you see. Always about awareness, always about contrast. The contrast you see today will be gone tomorrow and will reappear in three days. It does not make any difference at all. The path goes up and down and sideways and over rocks and under branches and uphill and downhill.

As soon as you sit down and face the wall, every step you take is completely unique. Just observe the six sense fields: the sense of touch, sense of taste, sense of thinking, smell, sound, sense of seeing. Everything is coming towards you, you could say. Just observe. If something begins to build up, just observe. If something begins to settle down or slide away, just observe. Whatever arises is exactly what it needs to be for you. There is nothing to correct. Only observe what arises. Don't go out towards anything. Allow everything to come towards you. Hold still without being rigid. Appreciate what occurs. Give room. Allow what occurs. Include what occurs. Just this.

As it is. (Bell)

Meditation Instruction #12

"I Vow to Be With All Things."

Please face the wall.

Here we find ourselves again at the beginning of, in this case, the all-day sitting. So the next two-and-a-half hours are basically what we call "block" sitting. This means just sit here and observe what arises in the six sense fields including the mind, including vision, sound, taste, touch and feeling. So every time we sit down and endeavor to practice shikantaza—just sitting, just precisely this—moment by moment by moment, we find ourselves in what has been called "beginner's mind." We don't exactly know what we're even doing. Coming back to square one. Coming back to this simple situation of just observing what is in front of us. The wall, the window, whatever is there. Not much.

So as we go along, as our mind goes along and as we endeavor to hold everything else very still in a gentle sort of way—not in an over controlling or rigid sort of way—just very gently sitting here, we take the attitude of just observing this. Whatever moves, observe. And when I say, "Observe," what I mean by this word is don't add to what you're seeing, feeling, touching, hearing with your comment, your opinion, evaluation, judgment or approval. Don't add to it or give it energy by looking away from it, ignoring it, or separating yourself from it thinking that in that way you can control your negative thoughts. Just observe. Very simply, whatever arises is just precisely that.

This is sometimes called "training" because it takes awhile to slowly, over time, see that if you do not feed the negative, positive, or neutral energy of the three poisons, if you do not add to them, push them down, agree with them, reject them, ignore them—if you do nothing with them—they begin to reveal themselves.

And they reveal themselves as what? Confusion, delusion, and ignorance.

As these emotions, movements, thoughts, memories, considerations, opinions, random thoughts, memories of the past, imaginations, projections, wishes for the future arise, just observe. As it says in the *Takkesage** which we chanted this morning—the first, short robe chant that we did—it says: "I *vow* to be with all things." I vow. I *will* be with things. I will take the attitude. I will become inspired by my willingness, by *this* willingness, by *a* willingness—regardless to whom it belongs—to be with all things.

If monsters appear in front of you, don't run, don't fight, and don't look away. If angels and other gentle, kind, seductive beings appear in front of you, do nothing at all. Don't accept them. Don't reject them. Don't look away from them. Just observe. Just look. A modern way of saying coming back to square one is Ctrl/Alt/Del. Just this. Simply start all over. Fresh start. Beginner's mind.

As Suzuki Roshi said: "In the expert's mind, possibilities are few; and in the beginner's mind, they are endless." Endless. Always begin. Always begin.

Just this. As it is. (Bell)

Takkesage (Robe Chant)

Dai sai gedap-puku muso fuku den e

Hi bu nyori kyo ko do sho shu jo

Great robe of liberation, virtuous field far beyond form

and emptiness, wearing the Tatagatha's teaching

We vow to be with all things.

Dai sai gedap-puku muso fuku den e

Hi bu nyori kyo ko do sho shu jo

Meditation Instruction #13

"Be Here And Observe."

Please face the wall.

Throughout the day, we accept, reject, exclude, include. Just as a reaction to whatever is arising, always a nuance of accepting, a nuance of rejecting or maybe a whole lot of it. And then maybe it might back off and then the thought that we shouldn't have gone that way so we move in the other direction. Always strategizing around our self-centeredness, around the assumption that we are a separate being who can succeed or fail, look good or look bad in other people's eyes. We project onto other people what they think about what we're thinking about what they're thinking about or what we're doing or what we're doing about what they're thinking about what we're doing. Very circular. Samsara.

We play that record over and over and over. We are not saying to stop it. We're not saying to increase it. We're not even saying to shut it off. We're saying just observe. Take this few moments out of your life, out of the circular activity, and hold still, and watch everything that continues to move. Notice the pattern. It rises, and it falls. And it rises, and it falls. Something cannot fall unless it has risen. Something cannot arise unless it has fallen. It's the very nature, the very relative nature of the world.

What you are doing when you hold still, sit still, have your hands in the cosmic mudra or on your knees if that is the way you need to sit, you are actualizing the fundamental point: Genjo Koan. You are actualizing— almost pretending to be—the absolute. You are accommodating, accepting, allowing things to arise and fall without adding anything to it. Without taking anything away from it. Very simply be here without any more strategy other than holding still and observing with all the senses open. See what occurs. See what occurs.

Watch yourself exclude. Don't try to stop that. Watch yourself include. Don't try to enhance that. Just observe.

If we were to take any direction at all, *any* direction at all, it would be to include. Just observe and see what this is fundamentally, for yourself. (Bell)

Meditation Instruction #14

"All Senses Are Welcoming."

Please face the wall.

Meditation instruction as it is taught here is hold the body very, very still without being rigid. All the senses are open, in particular the eyes. Hands are on your knees or in your lap with left hand over right, thumbs just barely touching forming an oval in what has been called cosmic mudra. Look directly at the wall. The wall itself may be heavily textured. Just look at those bumps, that texture. The idea is just to observe.

Hold the body very still, without being rigid. The body is upright, as if a string were gently pulling your head toward the ceiling, so your spine is slightly elongated. Very straight, but not rigid. Eyes are open. All the senses are open and welcoming. Be a good host.

Everything that arises, don't object. At the same time we don't object, don't necessarily agree. You don't have to do anything except observe. This is a training that goes back centuries and centuries.

Shikantaza, *just precisely this*. Moment by moment. Just watch your breath come and go—your heart beat. Feel the texture of your thoughts as they rise and fall. As they arise and pass by, like clouds in the sky. Clouds are very interesting, perhaps. Thoughts are very interesting, perhaps. The attitude we take toward clouds is the attitude we must take toward our thoughts as we practice shikantaza, zazen, or meditation. That attitude is *none of your business*. Clouds are none of your business. You have no sayso about clouds.

Thoughts, from the point of view of this teaching, are none of your business. Why? There really *isn't* anyone. There isn't a separate being anywhere. Wherever you look, wherever you see, feel, taste, touch, you will find not a separate person. Not a separate individual. There is only *this*, and you are not separate from it. Just observe. Whatever comes and goes. Whatever arises and falls. Whatever comes into view and passes out of view is just exactly what you need to see in this moment. Do not object, do not agree. Do not distract yourself or look away. Just this.

As it is. (Bell)

Meditation Instruction #15

"Stillness."

Please face the wall.

As simple as possible, this meditation called shikantaza or *just precisely this* is encouraging us to do something we don't do all day long. It's encouraging us to observe, see, experience in its fundamental nature, its fundamental texture precisely what is arising moment by moment in the mindstream or in any of the five sense consciousnesses. Just observe.

When we do this, we also experience the ways in which we can't quite do that, the ways in which we add onto what we see. Little comments. Add onto what we hear, add on with our commentary of feelings, emotions, memories, ideas. Just precisely this. So the encouragement is to use the body as a reference point.

Hold the body very still, and be aware, through feeling, that the body is just as still as you can make it, as you can encourage it to be. Hold very still and notice that there is still some kind of movement either in the body or in what we call the mind. Something is always moving along this way or that. Eventually, the stillness in the body, the lack of movement begins to inform the other senses, and we begin to see the stillness. Even in our thought patterns, we see the calmness at the same time our emotions are moving. We see the steadiness that consciousness displays by allowing things to arise and fall. No warfare. No taking sides. And even if we take sides, we notice that and stop doing it. Or it comes again, and we notice that, and then we stop doing it. Or maybe we keep noticing our movement over and over and over.

Whatever occurs in the mind or the sense consciousnesses, in order to practice shikantaza or zazen or *just precisely this*, we need to observe those sense consciousnesses. Awareness, thinking, feeling, remembering, hearing, smelling, tasting. We need to experience those first hand, one shot deal. It just occurs. We see it, and then we don't do anything with that. Just observe. In that way, even if we don't create the actuality of stillness, we create the attitude that seems to be required to hold completely still.

Whatever comes towards us as an emotion or memory or the freight train whistle we can hear in the distance— these experiences are just precisely this. If you do anything with it, then it is just precisely meddling. Just precisely pushing, precisely pulling. Don't add anything. Like sneaking up on a rabbit in the woods.

Just precisely this. (Bell).

Meditation Instruction #16

"Strengthen The Awareness Not The Thought Process."

Please face the wall.

Hold the body very, very still and just observe. All the senses are open, in particular the eyes. Look directly at a wall that is in front of you. Very simple. No designs. Just a blank wall. White. Gray. Light colored. Holding very still without being rigid, your head is erect as if a string were pulling you towards the ceiling slightly, straightening your spine but not being stiff.

This is called shikantaza which translates from the Japanese to *just precisely this*. The idea here is that we are going to look at whatever occurs in any of the six sense fields as just precisely this. In other words, no adding onto anything with our analyses, thought patterns, accepting, rejecting, ignoring. Anything other than just precisely this is adding.

And if we do find ourselves, through our awareness, adding onto something, if we notice something has arisen and we are very, very subtly putting a little tiny post-it note on that particular object of the senses whether thinking, taste, touch, smell, sound or sight—any little slight addition in terms of our idea about it—then just observe that. Step back a quarter of an inch to see what arises. Sometimes the arising is very simple, straightforward, and first thought. And sometimes there is that little extra push or addition that is a second thought. But if we see it, and if we don't continue to double up or laminate more ideas on top of that, then it remains simply just precisely this.

This is how we train ourselves to strengthen the awareness instead of the thought process. The thought process is already in charge of almost everything that happens in our life. In this situation of shikantaza, we are reprioritizing our thinking awareness process so that awareness begins to lead. Awareness begins to precede us in the sense that we see, hear, feel, taste, touch, even think very spontaneously in response to what is arising. What is arising. Not out of hope and fear that creates a situation where we are always wanting to be in control. Always wanting to be safe. Always wanting to be in charge. This in-charge feeling may help us somewhat. But fundamentally, the only real sanity is in awareness itself and not strategies or stories.

Hold the body very still, eyes are open. Look directly at the wall in front of you. Feel your body, and be open to what arises.

Just observe. (Bell)

Meditation Instruction #17

"Space."

Please face the wall.

Fifteen minutes before sitting begins, before the sutras are chanted, before the evening service, the morning service, we hear the sound of the han. We hear the strike on the wooden fish, and we notice the spaces between those strikes. We hear the temple bell, and we notice the sequence and the intervals. We notice the strikes. We notice the rings. We notice our mind, and we notice what we are doing at that time. Doing dishes. Using the restroom. In all of these situations, we notice the space between events, between strikes and rings and gongs and thoughts in our mind and the texture of the thoughts.

Without space you have no texture. You have solidified space. So we begin to notice the spaces, the intervals between things as we come into the zendo, into the meditation hall. We notice the interval, the space between what we were doing and what we are about to do. We come to the cushion and sit down, and we notice the space in front of us. The space in the zendo. The space between ourselves and others. And as we chant the sutras, we notice the spaces there between words, between sounds, between drumbeats. Just observing all of this. And when we turn and face the wall, we notice the space between the wall and our eye organ, between the wall and our body space. And that spaciousness also appears in the form of the interval between thoughts, emotions, feelings, memories.

Sometimes there's too much space that occasionally can be registered or named as boredom. We want something in the space. Or perhaps there are too many things going on, too many monkeys jumping, hollering. Not enough space. Always wanting something different. Holding the body very, very still, we observe that spaciousness in so many ways. The physical space, the mental or space in consciousness, in awareness and just the way in which it manifests and the way we see it in terms of the things, the thoughts, ideas, that arise in that space. Our expectations about things and the space between the expectation and its fulfillment or its absence. More space and our attitude could be just see this space, see this ongoing awareness.

It has been said that space and awareness are not dissimilar, that awareness is there so that things may occur in it. Trees. Plants. Sky. Branches, leaves. Frogs. Ducks. Amoebas. Paramecia. They arise, and they fall. Like we arise as this form, and we fall. Just observe. What arises and what falls and the space in which that occurs—just observe. Holding the body very still without being rigid, all the senses open, notice the space in every one of the senses. Without space, you have no item, no occurrence, no object. When thoughts of gaining and losing, accepting, rejecting, picking and choosing occur, simply look at the space in which that occurs rather than trying to get rid of that, accept that, reject that, judge that. Notice the spaciousness of everything.

Holding the body very still, observe that which continues to move—if anything moves at all. (Bell)

"Meditation Doesn't Work #1"

Notes from Sokuzan's Talks

Often, meditation is taught as a way of calming down, pacifying, stabilizing the mind, even creating another state of mind that is somehow tranquil and at peace. But Buddhist meditation as I understand it, and as it has been taught down through the centuries, is about *actually* seeing what we are *fundamentally* rather than pacifying what this body/mind complex *apparently* is. Because of this, meditation practice doesn't work—at least not in the way you *think* it's going to work.

Typically, we may use meditation to be a better person, a good meditator, to be more relaxed, get rid of this, get rid of that, to try to stop being angry or too passionate, too greedy, to be more aware, more mindful—all of which may occur in the context of your practice—but the process of meditation opens up the very shield or barrier you've been developing as protection against reality, like a finely woven matrix of your stories, opinions, ideas, judgments constantly invented, imagined, positioned, and strategized by the mind to get ahead in the world or get what we want, keep away what we don't want, and not be bothered by that which doesn't concern us. You might discover in your own situation that you don't like that. It's too uncomfortable. You feel more confused than ever.

When we practice shikantaza, the Japanese word for *just precisely this,* and hold the body very still allowing the six sense fields—sense of seeing, sense of sound, sense of smell, sense of taste, sense of touch, even the sense of thinking—to settle down and receive what's coming in: the sound of a bell; the fragrance of incense; a flower on the altar; sense of touch like the weight of our body in a chair or cushion; the taste of coffee, tea—this is an opportunity to take a few moments out of our day—ten minutes, twenty minutes, an hour or two—and just observe what this body/mind complex is doing.

When you sit down as the particular individual you are, you are introduced to your mind. You may have a pleasant experience, a neutral experience, a negative experience. But the most important thing you can hear from this old man is whatever comes, just receive it. Receive it with a sense of openness and intelligence. If it's very painful to sit there, don't do anything with it. Don't meddle with what arises. When I say, "Don't meddle," insofar as you're able, just look at whatever arises without pushing on it—judgment; without pulling on it—passion; or explaining what it is or telling a story around it. Don't add anything. Don't do any math when you're sitting. It's almost like a forensics scientist. He or she would look with bare attention to only what's there. Don't meddle with anything. Just look at it. *What is that?* is the question to ask. *What is that?* Not *why* is that. What's really important is just look. Just observe.

But if meditation doesn't work, why sit here? Why do this? Why sit here and subject yourself to this? When you sit down and hold the body still for any length of time, you start to see. Because you are still, you start to see everything that moves. And what moves? The mind.

The nature of the mind itself is continuous movement mostly in the service of self centeredness. You actually have to see it in order to stop seeing it. When you sit, you take the "food processor mind" that is constantly running, chopping, chopping, chopping, and pull the plug.

Q. Meditation is not always relaxing, is it? Can it be excruciating?

Sokuzan: Meditation, if we hold still, hold the body still for half an hour, an hour or more and take the attitude of just observing what arises, your particular situation may not be so relaxing. Some people may say, "This is pretty good. I haven't thought of doing this, of just sitting here and doing nothing." Depending on the causes and conditions of your personal karma, your own particular emotional, intellectual, psychological dynamic, your conditioning, your heredity—it's like looking at an oak tree, a maple tree that we know what it is but whose roots cannot be seen. We can't see where it gets its nourishment to be the very tree that it is. Same thing with our lifetime. We can find some cause and effect, why I was treated this way: I didn't have a good childhood, therefore I'm having emotional problems. We can trace some of that down, but quite often the causes and conditions that lead up to this present moment for a particular person are unfindable. There are just too many. Go look in the mirror and ask yourself, "How did *this* occur?" Other than your exact mother and father, you cannot find out how this happened. How did they get here? Because of their parents and on and on. All the causes and conditions and the buffeting we get on a daily basis. It is sometimes said if you want to know what your past life was like, look at your body. If you want to know what your future life will be, look at your mind because you are creating it moment by moment. This is already solidified, you could say, or caught in time. This particular karma.

Meditation doesn't work the way you think it does, but it does work in a way that you will discover as you do it. It will become very, very personal—so personal that, if you do enough of it, you won't be able to tell anyone about it.

Someone will say three years from now, "So, I hear you've been meditating. What do you do that for?" You'll probably say you're not really sure. If you find yourself saying that, you're doing it correctly from my point of view. It's so basic, so under the radar of discovery or logic. It's so foundational, so *under* the foundation, that it's about awareness itself not about ideas of right or wrong or something you can sell. So foundational. Very powerful. I highly recommend it. And if you've been meditating for three weeks, three months, three years, and feel like crap, you need to talk to someone like me. Perhaps not me in particular but someone who has done this for awhile. I've been practicing this for over forty years and have been reading about it for fifty years.

What I can tell you is—you don't have to become a Buddhist, but then some people need to glue themselves to this practice, and some people don't. They can meditate a little bit each day and do something else and come back to meditation, but it's very personal. Only you will know. No one can tell you to do this. It is only your decision or your intention, your motivation around that. It's not a belief system. Buddhism is not about believing in something. It's also not about disbelieving. It's about no position.

This is what you are doing when you sit. You are coming as close as you can to taking no position. Just this. You're not even a Buddhist. You don't even have clothes. No particular "I'm a boy, I'm an old man, I'm a woman." No reference points. You're just here. Use all your senses. You're just hearing. Smelling. Tasting. Just thinking. Thoughts go by like clouds. Clouds are none of your business. If you can take an attitude towards your own thinking process that it is none of your business, then this is beginning to approach the egolessness that the Buddha talked about. There is no separate self anywhere. Sure looks like it. Looks like I did this. I did that. I'm the one that has the headache. What is all this stuff about egolessness? It's the headache that has a headache. You don't really need a reference point of "me." You can function just fine without that. In fact, you function even better because hope and fear and worry about what people think is nearly gone, if not minimized. You're not operating out of what people think of you.

Q. You talk about there's nothing to correct, but we're unhappy about something or realize something is not right. It seems there is something to correct. What does it mean?

Sokuzan: I'm saying there are things that if we could change them we would, but if we take the attitude of correcting, it is jumping the gun. In other words, we're so anxious to correct that we try to change things before we see what it is. So when I say there's nothing to correct, this is path quality. It's how you practice it. Give me an example of what you would like to correct.

Q. I would like to be more disciplined.

Sokuzan: O.K. So the way that would be worked with rather than just try to be more disciplined is to *see* the way in which you *aren't* disciplined. It takes time. To actually look at that with that in mind when we're meditating—"Hmmm. How do I do this? Let's see. . .let me contemplate that." When you're sitting, just sit, just observe. And then maybe in post meditation you could make a list. You could work on it in a conceptual, intellectual way. So it's not about correcting it, but how does it show up that I'm *not* disciplined? You could do that. Or not. You could take a "soft" approach to it like taking an inventory. You could also bear in mind that is one of the things you are not clear about and see how that is. Takes time. Sit a lot.

To try to go at that concern with hammer and tong and change it, you know it doesn't work like that. You can't crowd yourself. One of the reasons we have this setup here is to for practitioners to come and practice with others like on the last Saturday of the month. It's very hard to sit by yourself. So we have a doan to keep time, and you can have someone sitting next to you. Then the gong rings; it creates a structure or a form. You can actually create that form for yourself by writing down when you're going to do things. Put it on your refrigerator or your bathroom mirror, and see if that would help you. Only you would know. So it's not about correcting. It's about being aware of how you're undisciplined. Seeing how that shows up rather than going in and trying to correct things.

Q. It's not so easy to see.

Sokuzan: No. The three poisons in Buddhism— aggression or trying to get rid of or destroy something. There's passion or generating ideas and stories around something, grabbing at things, pulling things, manipulating things, seducing things. Passion. We're not trying to get rid of passion. We need some emotion and feeling. I like ice cream. It's part of being a human being. But when it takes over and becomes greed or when ignorance, the third poison, takes over and becomes so cloudy that we don't see, when we get a flash every now and then of our lives, which may not be very good, and most of the time I'm just in the clouds about it and not thinking about it, I don't even see when I reach to pick up a coffee cup, take a sip, and then set it back down, I don't see where I'm going to place it. I'm lost in some daydream about what people think of me, what I think of me.

Meditation Doesn't Work #2

Notes From Sokuzan's Talks

So tonight, since we have a small group and several people are new to sitting meditation, I'll talk about a contradictory topic. Let's call it "Meditation doesn't work." Meditation doesn't work. And what's being said is that meditation doesn't work in the way you presume that it will. You meditate for three days, three weeks— you are always evaluating. The whole process of meditation is to slowly back off, deprioritize, or stop fueling the evaluation that is constantly going on: What will be advantageous for me? What will not be so good for me? How can I get ahead in this world? How can I get what I want? How can I keep away what I don't want and not be bothered by what doesn't concern me?

Meditation doesn't work according to your preconception about what meditation is or will do. This is not to say that if you hold very still and do various techniques that you won't be very relaxed. Sure, you may be. The problem is if you meditate in a way that is meant to relax you, you'll get relaxed. What's wrong with that? Wouldn't it be great to be relaxed? "I'm so relaxed when I meditate. I feel great. So wonderful. Like floating on a cloud. You should try it."

The problem with that approach is that you cannot do this while people are cutting you off in traffic. You cannot do this when your girlfriend, wife, husband is cheating on you. You cannot do this when you just lost the job that you really wanted. You cannot do this—use meditation to create another state of mind that is somehow tranquil, peaceful, at peace like the fourth mark of existence—the last one the Buddha saw was a monk who represented nirvana or tranquility or enlightenment.

On the other hand, meditation as it is being taught here, shikantaza or just sitting, means take everything you can hold still without force, take everything your body, speech and mind, everything you can hold still, and watch what continues to move. *Everything* keeps moving. There is very little you can hold still. If you hold your body still, there is blood flowing; there is breath; there is the movement of your changing body temperature that is measured by the sense of touch. Even the window rattles because it is vibrating to the resonance of the traffic outside or when you strike the drum in here during the sutras.

The nature of the mind itself is continuous movement but mostly in the service of what? Self centeredness. Me and my stuff. What I would like to get. What I'd like to keep away. What I'd like to control. What doesn't seem to have anything to do with me. You actually have to see the nature of the mind thoroughly in order to understand how it is self-perpetuating and lives off its own circularity. If you don't see the circular energy of it—samsara—you'll continue to assume direct cause and effect and miss seeing the interdependence of everything, which leads to the belief that we can somehow get control.

So meditation does not work in the way we think it will. But if you do *a lot* of sitting practice of meditation as it is being taught here, a *lifetime of it*—not just three weeks, three months, six months for a half hour a day—holding still and endeavoring to *just observe,* you actually relax into what you do. Then, when you have an action, it's actually genuine. You are actually in a genuine relationship with others not based on what *you* want or what you *don't* want or what you can ignore or control.

This does not mean, however, that you don't have feelings and emotions. It just means you don't necessarily act on them out of the impulsiveness of hope and fear that is blind to the truth. Emotions can be even more intense if one has begun to see that there is not a separate being here in the form of a centralized identity. There is identity, but it does not point to—or reinforce— separation. Therefore, the impetus is to experience emotions deeply with a sincerity that resonates with the present moment. Quite often, people who meditate a lot are asked, "You seem to be quite ruffled. Don't you meditate a lot?" *Yes, I have meditated.* "Well, you seem to be bothered by this. I thought a meditator wouldn't be bothered by anything. Apparently, meditation doesn't work."

Let's cut to the chase here. What is meditation? Why sit here? Why do this? Why sit here and subject yourself to this? Sometimes I and other teachers refer to meditation as "voluntary suffering" or "voluntary stress." In other words, when you sit down and hold the body still for any length of time, you start to see everything that moves. And what moves? The mind. And when you're not sitting, you're moving around, and it's easier to ignore what is arising because you are involved in pouring tea or moving across the floor or lighting a cigarette or popping into your car or looking down the clothes rack to see what you're going to buy in a store or answering the phone or fixing lunch or talking to your kids or talking to your grandmother—all ways of distracting yourself.

Q. Should we be stopping our daydreaming?

Sokuzan: No.

Q. So what should we do?

Sokuzan: Observe. Train yourself to prioritize observation over thinking. Don't try to stop thinking. Don't try to stop daydreaming. Don't do anything with it. It is very, very difficult to have thought patterns that are completely chaotic and radical and difficult and challenging and even scary and not try to *do* something with them especially stop or justify them.

One of the ways we stop thought patterns is to explain why it's happening: "Well, I must be thinking about this because Uranus is transiting over my natal Mercury in the fifth house. Or the moon is squaring my Saturn." Explaining why something is happening is called ignoring, a very active and structured way that is combined with passion, or trying to fluff things up, instead of sinking deeply through your awareness into the texture of that emotion, instead of allowing yourself to see it without a story—very difficult to look at something without a story that has emotional dynamics.

It's always about awareness. Always. Always. Always. ALWAYS about awareness. This does not mean you should stop thinking, stop your erratic behavior, your thoughts—anything. If you think this is about control, you are misguided. It's not true. It's about awareness of what control actually is. I can touch this coffee cup. Is that control? A little bit. What part of it is not control? I didn't create my hand. I didn't create that. I didn't create the space in which this occurs. Awareness sees that, and slowly we begin to see through the illusion of a separate self or ego.

So regarding your question, this is why it's so important to not meddle with anything that arises in the mind. It's like a forensic person on the scene of a crime. They don't touch anything. They come in, and they look. If there is a corpse there or if things are thrown around or a waste can turned over, they are very, very careful not to disturb the evidence. We train ourselves to just observe the little tiny details that come up as they arise. We train ourselves to just observe that. When erratic thoughts come up from the past or from wherever, we just watch them go. It's like clouds in the sky floating by. So when we have daydreams, we're just aware. You might even think, "I'm daydreaming—not a problem." But even the comment *I'm daydreaming* is a thought, and awareness needs to see that. The path part of it is Awareness backs up slightly and sees, and backs up slightly and sees, backs up slightly and so you get a little bit bigger picture. Less me. More that.

Q. I've heard you say there's nothing to fix. Some people come to meditation trying to fix themselves. Could you say what you mean when you say there's nothing to fix?

Sokuzan: I'm not saying we don't have issues or problems or a bad temper or that we don't worry or have any one of the passions—jealousy, anger, frustration, lack of self esteem, being kind of down on yourself, feeling guilty. We could go on and name all different levels of how that works. And what is being said here is usually the way this is treated in the Western world—and quite often in the spiritual world in theistic approaches or in therapies, is that there is something wrong. And we need to fix it.

It's taking the basic assumption that there is *somebody*. Just because there is a body/mind complex here with eyeballs and ears and a tongue and you can hear words coming out does not mean there is a separate individual happening here. Something's happening, but what is it? What is it? Do you know? *It's not separate.* So when this situation is seen through or we begin to see there isn't a solid being here, then the emotions, the feelings, intelligence are operating how? Orchestrated with everything else. Your feelings are no longer your own. Finally you realize you have no control at all. Over anything.

So, rather than becoming more disciplined, more controlled, more macho, nothing-ever-bothers-you, you meditate all the time so you never get upset, instead, what happens is you are completely genuine, sincere, and you meet everything where it's at.   If you can't meet this world *as it comes to you*, then you will separate yourself. By what? Judging—those people are bad. These people are good. I'm doing well. They're not doing so good. They're doing really well. I wonder why I'm not doing so well.

Q. What's the difference between meeting the world where it's at when it comes to you and creating karma?

Sokuzan: Simply put, things occur, and we judge that. Something occurs, and we jump to conclusions about it: "Well, this shouldn't be going on. He shouldn't be saying that. They shouldn't be doing this." Or if it's your own situation, something occurs and you have feelings, emotions, and you say, "I shouldn't be thinking that." A constant addition of little, tiny post-it notes on everything. If you just walk through a restaurant from one end to the other—do it as an experiment sometime— walk through a restaurant to the restroom and back to your seat, and see what your mind does. It adds and subtracts. In other words, values and devalues.

Q. What about if your mind doesn't do that? What if you just find yourself doing something, and your mind is barely involved? What if it's more of an emotional quality than a mind thought process?

Sokuzan: As my Teacher, Chögyam Trungpa Rinpoche said, emotions are just high-speed thoughts. They're just energized. The whole conceptual structure goes up and starts to be subjective, whereas in the thought process, it seems like there is an object—there's a window, a wall, there's a plant. As soon as you start to say, "I don't like that plant," then we're sliding out of the concept into the emotional area.

Q. So any overpowering emotion is just creating karma?

Sokuzan: Something occurs; there is some kind of emotion that arises out of *you* about that—first feeling, best feeling. In other words, the first spontaneous arising is what needs to be not meddled with. So you don't meddle with what's arising, and you don't meddle with your reaction to it. Through awareness, you actually see that you are meeting that. You are meeting that with something. A really good example of that is you're sitting on a park bench watching some kids on skateboards. One of the children falls, hits his knee, and falls down on the concrete. You can feel that through your whole body. You identify with how it would feel to have your knees hit that concrete. You see it. You're not going to sit back and say, "Well it's not happening to me." In other words, you meet it exactly where it's at. Any thought beyond that is adding. Anything that comes up spontaneously is coming out of the karma that is already here. You already are a human being.

Q. It seems impossible in this world to not *do* anything. Even when you *don't* do something, it's doing something.

Sokuzan: What you're describing here is *awareness*. You have the *awareness* that it seems impossible to do something because even when you're not doing something, you're doing something. That's awareness. You can't talk like that unless you have awareness.

Q. You can't *not* do anything.

Sokuzan: That's awareness.

Q. Can you stop the flow of karma? Can you hop out of your karma?

Sokuzan: No. What can you do? See that it's not real. And the only way you can see that it's not real is to completely, fully, totally feel it. You *have* to feel it. Because if you sit back and *say* it's not real, you've separated yourself from it and have a story about it: Oh, that's not real. Form is emptiness. Emptiness is form. The same is true of feeling, perception, memory, and consciousness. People are doing this with the Heart Sutra and other emptiness teachings, sitting back away and saying, "Oh that's empty. It's not real. It's a dream. An illusion." I'm not saying you shouldn't think about that, but the question you asked me—Is it possible to step out of that? No, not separate. It's called compassion. One actually has to feel very, very deeply whatever arises. You *have* to feel it.

Q. Is there a point where you become aware of your karma and you may not want it but part of you wants it because of some reason you don't even know why you want it. But a part of you doesn't. What do you do?

Sokuzan: You're actually describing the split. Anytime you hear someone say, "A part of me wants . . ." If you bring that to me, this is just a division.

Q. How do you address the division?

Sokuzan: Be aware. You have to *see* it. And you cannot do anything with it. You have to see that you are dividing yourself. If you think there's a fork in the road, then you're wrong. If you think there is more than one direction to go, then you're actually dividing things up.

Q. What if there is a lot of fear?

Sokuzan: You've heard me say, "Don't do anything unless you *have* to do it." When I say *have* to, this doesn't mean that just because you *want* to—if you have an addiction situation, it's because you *want* to smoke cigarettes or have a drink—you just don't do that. It's very personal. I think if you have a strong sitting practice, a strong meditation practice, then you'll begin to see—and, of course, there's no guarantee because everyone's karma is different—then you'll begin to see when you start to step into something. You see your motivation for why you're doing something you don't have to do. If you don't have to do that, it means you're operating out of passion, aggression, ignorance, hope, and fear. Anytime you're operating out of hope and fear—fear that things are going to get worse, hope that they're going to get better—this is a misunderstanding of how things work.

Q. Do you not believe we have the choice of doing something good or something bad?

Sokuzan: I think it's a very touchy area, and the way in which it's difficult is, if you see two choices, *this looks good; this looks bad,* if you see that, the problem is that instead of seeing what this actually *is in toto*, you actually see your *idea* about it. Based on your conditioning, your past, how you've been treated, how you think, what your own personal fears are, what's in it for you, how you would look if you did that, what would people think if you did that--"I'm so drawn to that; I'm not going to be able to stop myself! Here I go! What are people going to think?"

So what do we do with that? We actually have to become our own authority. Fundamentally, you have to become your own authority. And that's very risky because it means you're dropping out of the status quo of human beings that live like lemmings. They follow the status quo except when they're in private then they do what they want. They think nobody's watching.

It's very important to strengthen or crank up or fuel the awareness. The space in which thoughts and thinking and ideas and opinions and emotions and memories arises—there is a space. For most people, it's like a closet. And it's like their closet is full of furniture, and you can't even lie on the couch because it's standing on end in the closet. So it's unusable. And if you ask someone a question that takes any sense of brainpower or acumen or some kind of ability to discriminate between this and that, you'll see people immediately go into opinions. Very difficult for most people to talk freely out of the understanding of what's there. They'll say, "I've always thought. . .I was taught. . .Well, that's wrong. What do you think?" "Yes, I think that's wrong, too." Most conversations are swapping opinions.

Q. It's a hard concept to grasp—awareness—without analyzing it.

Sokuzan: Go ahead and analyze, but be aware that you are analyzing. How do I know this? I do it all the time. I could not teach this or talk about this if I had not had seventy-two years of experience with it including forty years of sitting on a cushion looking at my mind. So I would say to you, continue to live the way you live, continue to think, continue to make decisions, continue to jump the gun or not, continue to manipulate your mind or not, just strengthen the awareness so that you can get more and more clear about the way in which you create problems for yourself. Because we do it. We create stuff. Not even to talk about the stuff that comes out of our past karma, you know, the train wreck that we run into. Not to talk about three weeks down the road when your closest friend dies.

The kind of control modality that most therapies, even spiritual paths, is not going to help you with that. The only thing that will help you with that—from this old man's point of view—is really strong awareness. Awareness that doesn't leave anything out. Awareness that never shuts the door on anything. The temptation to shut the door on oncoming pain is very, very strong. It takes a lot of bravery to look at a train coming at you, something you see that is inevitable, that is going to happen and not shut down on it. Very hard to do that. Sometimes we shut down, and we don't even know we're shutting down because we have such a warp and woof—to use a weaving image—of our ideas about why we shouldn't do that. "Well, if that happens. . .if he does that. . .then I'm not going to do that. . ." It's just a constant generation of ideas and opinions that keep us from living our life.

You should live your life so that it's just like going down a slide. You get on that slide and you go! And all I'm saying is *turn up the awareness*. And if you do, you'll see that everyone is experiencing this life as a little tiny being that thinks he or she is somehow separated from everything else. Not true. You are not separate. And when you begin to see that, you live. It doesn't mean you're going to stop suffering. It doesn't mean you're suddenly going to have a halo around your head, that people are going to love you. In fact, you might be more cranky than ever.

So I would say strengthen the awareness so that you can see the truth for yourself, so that you can be your own authority. So that you don't have to look outside of yourself to see if you are right or wrong. And what does that awareness do? It shows you that "right" and "wrong" is a relative idea. There is no such thing. If you live out of right and wrong, then you'll be in warfare with yourself the rest of your life. Or with your neighbors or with your psychiatrist or your priest. We have to do it ourselves.

So meditation doesn't work. The idea of sitting down and training the mind to actually see does not work in the way that we think it's going to work. It works. But it works in a way that if you knew ahead of time the way in which it was going to work, you probably wouldn't start meditating. Sorry to tell you that.

Q. How does it work?

Sokuzan: Over time, if it's done correctly—in other words, with as little as possible, as simply as possible— as the Danish theologian, Soren Kierkegaard said, "Purity of heart is to will one thing." Will *one* thing. Be completely genuine. Totally straightforward. Just this. *Just this*. And if whatever comes and looks like *just this*, then don't deviate from it. Don't deviate. In other words, in paraphrasing Kierkegaard, if you will the good, completely good, and look for a result, this is double-mindedness or twoness or suffering. In the Buddhist idea, *dukkha*. And Kierkegaard is saying, just do this. Just do good. Just the truth. If I do the truth, will I be getting better?

So this situation of meditation practice fundamentally strengthens that which fundamentally sees the truth. You *can* see the truth for yourself. And the truth put in relative terms is *not separate*. You can actually see that. It is not an experience. Hearing the sound of this bell is an experience. Do you know how I know it's an experience? It's gone. Where did that sound go? You heard it, but it's gone. Everything is vanishing into emptiness, impermanence. Everything you are looking at right now will be gone including your own body/mind complex.

Q. Do you think living to will one thing is meeting the world where it's at?

Sokuzan: Maybe. Find out. Trust yourself. When I say that, I'm not saying trust your thoughts, your opinions, your ideas or all the furniture in the closet, I'm saying trust the space inside the closet. Without that space, nothing would be happening. And if you trust that space, for some unknown reason, the space suddenly—instead of being a closet, the walls fall over and the space opens up into a field, a meadow, an open dimension. And there may be things in it or not. But you don't mind. There's a pool table over here. Someone is sliding down a pole over there. Maybe a black cloud here, a white cloud there. You don't mind. If something comes walking towards you in that space, you have a lot of time to consider what it is. What is that called: A lot of time to consider what it is? One really well-known word we all misunderstand. Patience. Wait until it gets to you. Wait until the fork in the road gets to you, and then you'll see that there actually is no fork. There is only one way to go, and that's what Kierkegaard is talking about.

Q. So if there is no "self," and you say to trust yourself, is that trusting that space?

Sokuzan: It is. You are trusting the space in which apparent things occur. In trusting that space, you may find yourself attaching or rejecting or accepting things that occur. Don't worry about it. Don't push away the things so you can have more space. This is called paranoia. Just be with whatever arises without accepting, rejecting or ignoring—not so easy.

Q. How do you know when you're doing that?

Sokuzan: You won't know. If you know, you're not doing it. You won't know. There is a sense of not being separate from things. So you may find yourself resonating like the window when things roll down the street making a lot of racket. You may make a lot of racket also. The idea is to always be genuine. If you're genuine, then you're not sitting in judgment of yourself or anyone else. You may feel like it. Not so easy to do.

In simple terms it comes down to *just this*. What you are looking for you are looking at. You might say, "Well, I'm looking at the carpet. Are you saying that's what I'm looking for?" In a sense, yes. You're actually looking at yourself. Now, the carpet may not be as interesting as looking at a wheelbarrow full of gold bullion or strawberry shortcake . How do we train to do that? We train by looking at the wall, looking at the floor, just sitting down, holding still, training our minds so that we can begin to understand that. It's not easy to do.

And everyone's karma is arising as some kind of story out of the past. We're meeting things so when something comes up, we meet it with our response, our action. And it seems that the more we meditate, the more clear we are on what we should go along with and what we shouldn't go along with. We're just more clear on it. You might say if we're not clear, should we do anything? No. Don't do anything unless you have to. Reflect on this for a minute: if you do something you don't have to do—I'm not saying if something happens and you have an emotional response about that, you can't help that, you can't stop that. But you may have some sayso about what you do about that emotional response. Or not. You may have an emotional response and blurt something out in anger. If you do, you do.

Sometimes, in the Buddhist tradition, there are all kinds of warnings about that. In fact, there is a precept about that: don't get angry. I don't like that precept because some people can't help but get angry. They get angry. That doesn't make them wrong. Some say they are breaking a precept because they got angry. No, I'm afraid that you, in saying that to them, don't realize the kind of karma that they had to deal with even to get to a cushion where they could experience their anger.

Insofar as you can, don't do anything unless you have to because when you do something you don't have to, you are starting to create more karma. It may be very good karma.

Q. So is there a goal to wear out the karma you have and not create more karma?

Sokuzan: Yes.

Q. Why?

Sokuzan: Suffering. Not only the suffering of this person, this apparent individual, but the suffering of others. We have a little bit of suffering, but it's backed off enough that we can actually come to a Zen Buddhist temple and meditate and ask questions. Or I can sit up here and talk. But the reason we do it is the same reason the Buddha did: to relieve suffering.

We may have two years, three years, eighteen years of relative peace, but at some point, this body will be a corpse. And those bodies around us will be corpses. Not to be negative, but it's just the truth. We don't know how we got here. We don't know if we could do this again. We don't know if we would even *want* to do it again. The first reminder says, "First, contemplate the preciousness of being free and well-favored; difficult to gain, easy to lose. Now I must do something meaningful." In this tradition, it means *sit down and look at your mind.* It doesn't say believe in Buddha, build a bunch of golden idols to Buddha, bow down, and worship things. It says, "Do something meaningful." Let's just see what is coming up all the time. Over and over. We respond. Something happens. We respond. Something else happens. We respond.

If you voluntarily sit down and do *nothing,* if you do nothing at all and just observe what happens, over time the awareness part of this whole matrix we call a living being starts to get strong enough so that your interaction with others is flooded with awareness. It does not mean you can change your karma. You cannot suddenly become a person who never has bad thoughts.

Q. Is there a way to tell the difference if you are creating karma or wearing it out?

Sokuzan: Some karma that comes up grabs you by the throat and drags you into it. Some of it. If you're doing your best as a practitioner using what we sometimes refer to as discipline by holding still and not doing anything unless you have to, then if you continue to do something, like Byron Katie says, "How do you know if you should be doing that? Because you're doing it." It's always about awareness. It's never about control. If you think it's about control, there is a big battle going on there.

Q. Yes, but you could be doing something and creating new karma?

Sokuzan: Yes, you can.

Q. So this *supposed to be doing it,* you are because you're doing it, but you still can't tell if you're supposed to because you're wearing that karma out?

Sokuzan: Insofar as I understand it, if you're doing something you don't have to do, then you are adding to karma. If you can refrain from reacting to something— I'm not saying you don't have a feeling dynamic with everything that happens—but if you can work with that as what it is without adding to it, then because you're not adding to it, the karma that is arising that causes that kind of situation doesn't get any fuel. If you do anything with it, then it's fuel. Not that it's wrong. It's just called samsara. It's a wheel. Then you get on another realm and another realm. That's why we build temples. That's why we have cushions. That's why we have a practice, chant sutras. We keep trying to glue ourselves to this teaching which says things are empty of what we think of them. And there is no self in the skandhas. The dualistic appearance of things is not true. This was discovered centuries ago and happens to be a spiritual path.

Q. Couldn't that be hiding out from your karma sometimes? You just hole up in a temple somewhere?

Sokuzan: If you need to hole up in a temple, like the gentleman upstairs who is in a ten-day strict solitary retreat, you'll have to do it. Other people may look at that and say, "Whew, why would I do that? I'm going to do something else."

Q. But couldn't you use that as an escape?

Sokuzan: You could. It depends on how you're working with your mind as you're doing that.

Q. To me, karma is just energy, right?

Sokuzan: Karma is a Sanskrit word that means *action*. If there is an action, there is a reaction. The air has to get out of the way for me to move this.

Q. So if I can choose how I'm working with my mind, can I choose the action of my karma?

Sokuzan: Probably not. The only real choice we have is awareness. Or hold your seat. The simple idea is, for example, my addiction to cigarettes. I haven't smoked in twenty years. But the way I worked with that is I just became stubborn about it. I desperately wanted to smoke cigarettes, but I knew if I wanted to keep *not* doing it when the little stories arose—"You haven't smoked in three weeks; you can just have one and then go back to quitting again; buy a pack and keep them in the trunk of the car"—a constant barrage of justifications of why I could have another cigarette—trying not to smoke but had this addiction to it. Eventually, I just stopped. It was a kind of stubbornness. I knew I had to stop it somehow because no one was going to do it for me. I'm not suggesting a technique here, but I just became very stubborn and made up my mind, you could say, to not smoke or I would be dead. It was going to kill me.

Q. Is that what you mean that there isn't a fork in the road? When you got to that point, you only saw the one way to stop?

Sokuzan: Seems that way, yes. The rest of the time I was trying to figure it out. It's almost like saying I couldn't quit until then.

The emphasis here is not about right or wrong. If you start thinking in terms of right or wrong, I should or I shouldn't, please, try to emphasize the awareness about the *qualities* of right and wrong. The awareness really needs to shine. It's hard to do that. It's especially hard to do it without training ourselves, training ourselves to not jump the gun. If you jump, depending on what it is, I'm not saying everybody should be afraid to do anything, I'm saying if you have a lot of awareness around it—"I don't really need to do that; I don't really need to quit my job; I don't really need to get a degree in computer science"—or like in our situation, if you don't need to come to this temple or meditate or study this material, don't do it. Do something else. There's no requirement. I'm not here to sell you anything.

The idea is to trust yourself. Trust the space in which thoughts and ideas and opinions arise. Trust the *space* in which thoughts arise—not the thoughts themselves. And if you do that, it doesn't have a dynamic to it. It just has a sense of openness where you have the courage to actually see intense feelings and emotions and thoughts come in and play, and you don't buy into them. Not easy. It takes a lot of courage because it's like saying isn't that like going into a "bad neighborhood?" If you go into a bad neighborhood, aren't you going to get contaminated? You might. One person I've worked with who has difficulty with that is it's not a matter of staying out of a bad neighborhood but being *aware* of that's what it is. The image I've used there is like a rattlesnake and a jelly doughnut. You can't take your eye off that rattlesnake for a minute. If you do look away, it looks like a jelly doughnut—and you *like* those. You think you'll just take a bite. You'll take a little bite because you've got a lot of self control. You'll be okay with this. Little mini stories coming out. And the next thing you know, you've got a rattlesnake in your mouth. And you wonder, while it's biting you, "How did I get this?"

Q. Do we create and wear karma out in the same lifetime?

Sokuzan: Using the concept of karma is tricky because it looks like we can get a hold on it. Am I wearing it out or building more? There's only one way: *you have to do it yourself.* No person—me functioning as a teacher or anyone else—can point it out for you. I kind of see it but know you can't hear me. If you come and ask me directly, I might be able to tell you. Come and sit in front of me and open up, then I can say something. I can help you. But if you don't, I can't say much especially about something like karma. I don't know what you need to experience. I don't know what you personally need to do, but if you're doing it, then that's probably what you need. Or not. That's why awareness is so important—to be aware of *what this is*. Not go to war with anything. If you're doing this at all, you just need to see it. You don't need to go to war with this. If you go to war with this then you have another fist coming down. Not easy.

Sokuzan's Basic Recipe

The Sitting Practice of Meditation or

Shikantaza: "Just Precisely This."

After over forty years, my study and practice of sitting meditation can be distilled to just precisely this: "Sit down, and look at the mind. Strengthen the Awareness of that which sees—not that which thinks." Although I do not promise becoming more peaceful, less aggressive, more loving, less suffering, I can promise this: you will never regret the time you have spent sitting down and looking at your mind. Good Luck!

Ingredients:
1 willing student who is inspired to see the truth for himself or herself
1 hour, more or less, of time
1 meditation cushion (or chair or bench)
1 quiet place with a blank wall
1 bell and striker (gong, glass of water and a spoon or chopstick, or other suitable instrument for initiating the sitting period; a snap of the fingers can also provide the starting and stopping sound)

Optional:
1 candle
1 stick of incense

1. Light the candle and incense, if desired.

2. Bow to the cushion; turn and bow to the center of the room, the world.

3. Sit down on the cushion facing the wall.

4. All the senses are open—in particular the eyes.

5. Strike the bell.

6. Place your hands either on your knees or in cosmic mudra with the left hand on top of the right, thumbs just barely touching forming an oval between your thumbs and first fingers.

7. Hold the body very, very still, back straight without being rigid as if a string were pulling you upward by the top of your head.

8. Just observe. Whatever arises in the six sense fields— the sense of sound, the sense of smell, sight, taste, touch, thought—just observe.

If you are holding very, very still without being rigid, all of your senses are open, and if you are endeavoring to just observe, you are doing this correctly. Whatever arises in your mind, don't add, don't subtract, and don't look away. Just observe. There is nothing to correct. There is nothing to adjust. There is just this. Just observe.

Bake for 1 hour, more or less, or until done. Strike the bell to end your sitting practice.

About The Author

Kyoun Sokuzan, head priest at SokukoJi Buddhist Temple and Monastery in Battle Creek, Michigan, is a fully transmitted monk in the Soto Zen Buddhist tradition. He met Chögyam Trungpa Rinpoche, a preeminent teacher of Tibetan Buddhism, in late 1973 and became a student. In 1974, Sokuzan attended the first session of Naropa Institute in Boulder, Colorado. In 1975, he established the Dharma Study Group of Battle Creek, Michigan, offering weekly meditation and study as well as monthly nyinthuns, or all-day retreats. In 1978, Sokuzan became an authorized meditation instructor through Vajradhatu in Boulder and later completed the Vajradhatu Seminary in 1980 at Lake Louise in Alberta, Canada.

In 1990, Sokuzan met Kobun Chino Roshi, a Zen meditation master from Japan, and became a student of his, receiving lay ordination from Kobun's brother, the late Hojosama Keibun Otagawa. Sokuzan received full ordination as a priest in the Soto Zen lineage in 2007 and Dharma transmission in March of 2013 from Kuzan Shoho Michael Newhall, Abbot of Jikoji in Los Gatos, California.